DO YOU MOVE AS I DO?

Written and illustrated by Helen Borten

The world is a never-ending ballet, full of movement to look at and enjoy. Every movement speaks of joy and sorrow, love and hate — gentle as rocking a cradle or violent as an explosion. Skip like an autumn leaf, feel the power of a hurricane. Move quickly like a shooting star soaring across the sky, or snuggle into the warm softness of a blanket on a winter's night. Move gracefully, like a skater gliding on the ice or a snake weaving to a snake charmer's flute . . . Jump, like "I'm so happy I can't stand still," or shrug like "I don't know . . . " Speak with your body as well as your voice. Movement can *do* something. It can *say* something, too.

*

Classification and Dewey Decimal: Psysiology (612)

About the Author and Illustrator:

HELEN BORTEN, author-illustrator, feels that a rich, cultural background in art and music is one of the most valuable gifts to give a child. The author attended the Philadelphia Museum College of Art. Her books have been chosen by the *New York Times* among the Ten Outstanding Books of the Year as well as the Ten Best Illustrated Books. Mrs. Borten divides her time between her family and her art work.

Do You Move
As I Do?

Do You Move
As I Do?

1966 FIRST CADMUS EDITION
THIS SPECIAL EDITION
IS PUBLISHED BY ARRANGEMENT WITH
THE PUBLISHERS OF THE REGULAR EDITION
ABELARD-SCHUMAN LIMITED
BY
E. M. HALE AND COMPANY
EAU CLAIRE, WISCONSIN

284

by Helen Borten

To Karl, Kenny, Harry, Diane and Margo

This edition lithographed in U. S. A. by Wetzel Bros., Inc., Milwaukee 2, Wisconsin

I see movement
everywhere around me.
Movement can *do* something—
like scrub my teeth or tie my shoe—
and it can *say* something too.
My finger pointing says, "Look!"
My hug says, "I love you."
My shudder says, "Ugh, I don't
like that."
When I jump up and down and
squeeze myself, my body is saying,
"I'm so happy I can't stand still."
My shoulders lifting in a shrug
say, "I don't know."
My bare toes wriggling in
the grass say, "How good this
grass feels!"
So you see, I "speak" with my
body as well as my voice.

When I awake, still deep in dreams,
I move slowly, oh so slowly until
my room seems real again. The quieter
I feel, the slower I go. Slow movement
may be as lazy as my yawn or as
thoughtful as an old man stroking his beard.
It can be as eerie as mist rising from
the earth or as heavy as a steam roller.

Sometimes slow movement is tender—
like Mother's fingers smoothing my hair.
Sometimes it is sad—like
a crippled bird limping in the snow.

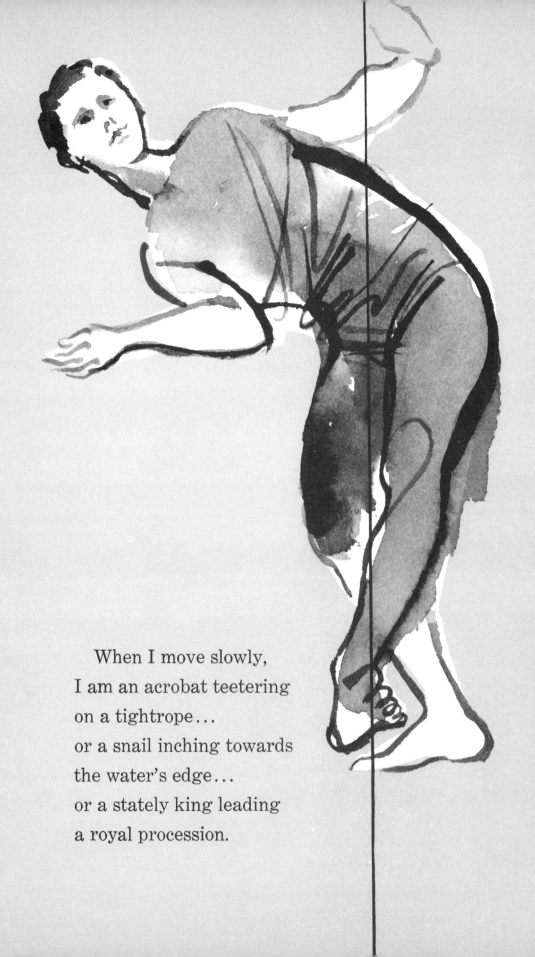

When I move slowly,
I am an acrobat teetering
on a tightrope...
or a snail inching towards
the water's edge...
or a stately king leading
a royal procession.

Sometimes I feel too happy to move slowly. So I skip as gaily as an autumn leaf in a gusty breeze. The more excited I feel the faster I move. I run so fast, I feel as light as a kite, as strong as the wind, as free as a bird. Fast movement can be as reckless as a stampede of wild horses and as powerful as a hurricane. It makes me feel as fizzy as ginger ale.

When I move quickly,
I am a swashbuckling swordsman

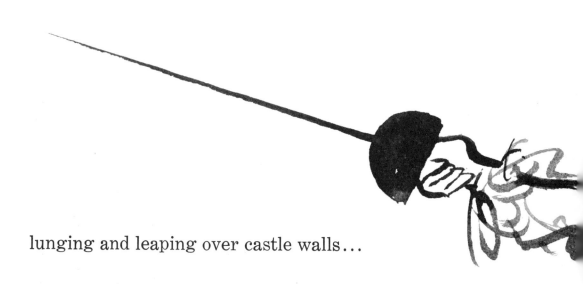

lunging and leaping over castle walls...

or a shooting star soaring across the sky.

When I snuggle into the warm
softness of my blanket on a winter night,
my body stretches and curls and
wriggles with pleasure—like a cat
being stroked. Long flowing movements
ooze as smoothly as honey and curve
gracefully, like a fountain making
patterns of beauty. I remember
throwing a stone into a pond and
watching the ever-widening circles
it made in the water.
Flowing movement pulls me into its
spell—like a whirlpool.
Sometimes it makes me want
to spin as merrily as a carousel.

When I move in a graceful,
flowing way, I am a skater
gliding on the ice...
or a snake weaving
to a snake charmer's flute...
or a willow tree rippling
in the wind.

When I am all dressed up
in party clothes and Mother
fusses with my hair, I jerk
and tug and yank and pull.
My whole body fidgets with
impatience. Short, jerky
movement is never round and
smooth like flowing movement,
but full of corners--
like a salute.
　　It explodes in a series of
sparks, like a pinwheel,
and makes me feel as frisky as a
jumping bean. It can be as sharp
as a kick or as twinkly as a wink.

Sometimes it makes me
squeeze up all tight inside,
until I feel like a cowboy
gripping the sides of a horse
that rears and bucks
under me.

When I move in a quick,
jerky way I am a mechanical doll...

or a clown stumbling over my own feet...
or a frantic fish
struggling on a fisherman's hook.

Sometimes my spirit leaps up
inside me and I am sure I can
do *anything*. If I were a bird I
would fly, if I were a ship I would
sail the highest waves. I rise up,
up, up on tiptoe and reach for the
nearest cloud. I climb to the top
of the tallest tree to sit in the lap
of heaven. Movement that goes up
may strive as mightily as Atlas,
lifting the world on his shoulders.
It can be hopeful—like hands
clasped in prayer, or proud—like
a boxer's arms raised in victory.

When I move upwards, I am a mountain
climber scaling the highest peak...
or a seed pushing up through the soil...
or a rocket soaring into outer space.

But when I am tired, I move in a droopy way.
My eyelids droop and my head droops, my arms
droop and my back stoops, until I feel as
limp as a rag doll. Movement that goes down
can be as sad as a tear, as humble as a bow,
or as crushing as an avalanche. It pulls me
down with it—like quicksand.

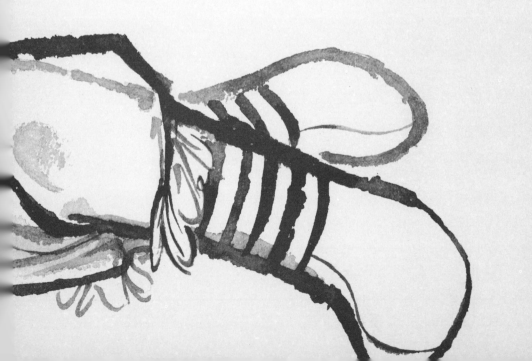

Crouching and drooping and crawling and
stooping make me feel as earthbound as
a turtle wallowing in the mud.

When I move downwards, I am a tree
felled by a woodsman's axe . . .
or a stone sinking to the bottom of a well.

When Daddy comes home from work, I dash forward eagerly to greet him. Forward-going movement can be open and giving, like my palm offering candy to a friend. But it can push and take too, like a child grabbing toys from his playmate. It can be as sassy as a stuck-out tongue, or as impulsive as a leap in the dark. It can be as bold as a punch in the nose, or as menacing as a tidal wave.

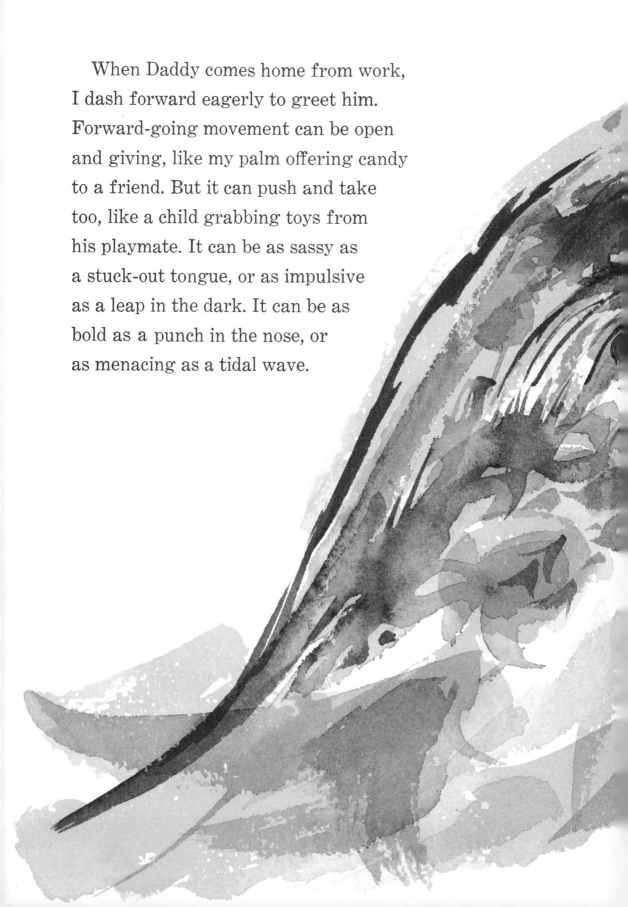

When I move forward,
I am a warrior marching into battle...

or an explorer
braving the unknown to discover new worlds.

But sometimes I am not so brave; I twist
my fingers shyly behind me and back away timidly
from something or someone new.

Backward-going movement can shrink in fear,
recoil in disgust, or spring back in surprise.
It can be as stingy as a miser's closing fist
or as cold and unsociable as an oyster
drawing into its shell. When I move backwards,
I am a cat cringing in terror...
or a flower closing its petals against the frosty night air.

So you see, sometimes movement
can say more than words.
    Dancing is rhythmic movement
that "speaks"—of joy and sorrow,
of love and hate, of hope and fear. It
can describe the world inside me and the
world around me. It can be as gentle as
the rocking of a cradle or as violent
as an explosion.

    A dance is like a poem—
and movements are its words.
    A dance is like a song—
and movements are its melody.

I see movement everywhere around me:
clouds drifting, eyebrows lifting,
flags waving, Daddy shaving, birds
worming, worms squirming, planes flying,
clothes drying, babies creeping,
willows weeping, faucets leaking,
and children hide-and-seeking.

I see the world as a never-ending
ballet, full of movement to look at
and enjoy. I am a dancer in that ballet—
and so are you.
Do you move as I do?

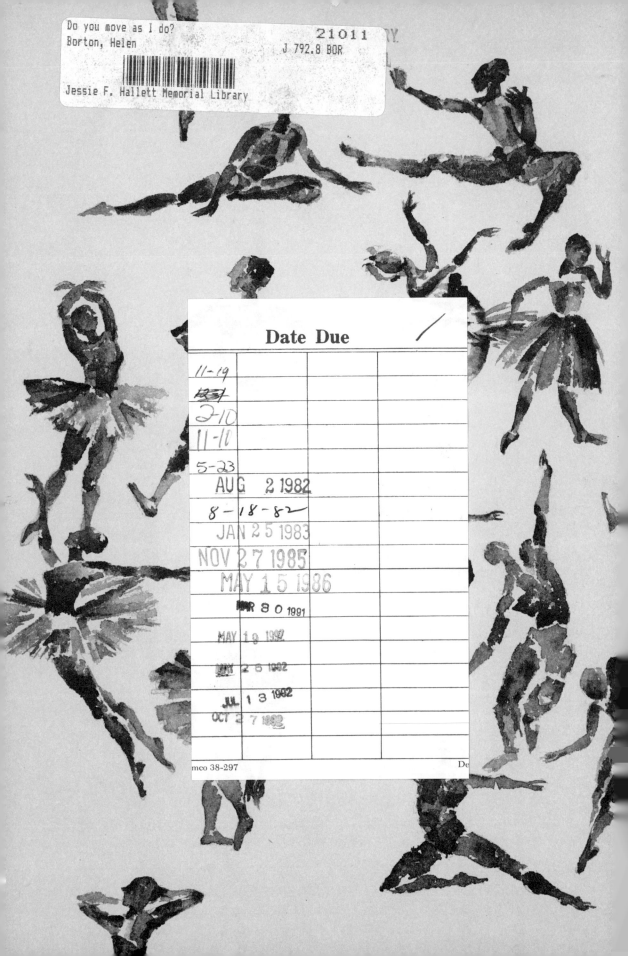

Date Due

11-19			
12-31			
2-10			
11-10			
5-23			
AUG 2 1982			
8-18-82			
JAN 2 5 1983			
NOV 2 7 1985			
MAY 1 5 1986			
MAR 3 0 1991			
MAY 1 9 1992			
MAY 2 6 1992			
JUL 1 3 1992			
OCT 2 7 1992			

mco 38-297   De